The Lighthouse Book

The Lighthouse Book

Samuel Willard Crompton

Photography by Charles J. Ziga

BARNES
& NOBLE
BOOKS
NEW YORK

This edition published by Barnes and Noble, Inc., by arrangement with Saraband (Scotland) Ltd.

2003 Barnes & Noble Books

Design © Ziga Design

Library of Congress Cataloging in Publication Data available

ISBN: 0-7607-4203-0

Printed in China

10 9 8 7 6 5 4 3 2 1

Page 1: Heceta Head Light (detail), Florence, Oregon; pages 2–3: Ram Island Ledge Light, Portland, Maine; these pages: Southwest Ledge Light, New Haven, Connecticut.

This book is for my father, Willard Crompton. Like a lighthouse, he sent light and comfort to everyone he met.

— SWC

Contents

The Evolution of the Lighthouse

Humans are torn between adventure and safety, the desire for comfort and the need for exploration. Lighthouses embody this tug and pull within the human spirit: the flashing beacon or resounding horn warns sailors of the dangers that lurk close at hand. The prudent mariner pays attention, but also knows that no amount of technology can ensure a safe passage and arrival.

The first lighthouse of which we have definite knowledge was that of Pharos, in the harbor of Alexandria, Egypt. Alexander the Great founded the city that bears his name on the extreme western side of the Nile Delta in 331 BC. One of Alexander's generals, Ptolemy Soter, became king of Egypt in 305 BC. During his reign, Ptolemy commissioned Sostratus of Cnidus (a city in southwest Asia Minor—present-day Turkey) to build a lighthouse in the harbor on the island called Pharos. The work was completed around 280 BC, during the reign of Ptolemy II Philadelphus (from 282 until 246 BC).

The Pharos was justifiably known as one of the Seven Wonders of the Ancient World. Built of stone, it was more than 400 feet tall, on a base larger than 300 square feet. Egyptians (slaves, probably) brought wood and dung that were burned to create a fire at the base: convex mirrors then reflected the sun's rays and created a beam visible as far as 33 miles across the Mediterranean Sea. The lighthouse was displayed on Greek Imperial coins cast at the Roman mint between AD 81 and 192. The Pharos was the largest and grandest lighthouse ever built by human hands.

In AD 641 Alexandria was captured by the Arabs. The Pharos was damaged in the siege and ceased to operate as a lighthouse. However, it remained a landmark for another 800 years. The structure was damaged still more by earthquakes that occurred in 956, 1303 and 1323, and by the mid-fourteenth century, it had fallen into ruin. Yet it remained vivid in the minds of men who wanted to devise a way to tame the ocean's fury and unpredictability. In 1995 a team of French archaeologists led by Jean Yves Empereur located many of the underwater remains of the Pharos in Alexandria's harbor. As their work continues at this writing, it appears that archaeology will verify the legendary splendor and size of the Pharos Lighthouse.

The Romans had built lighthouses along the coasts of Spain, France and southern Britain, but as the Roman Empire succumbed to the power of the Germano-Norse tribes, the beacons fell into disrepair, and few scientific advances were made. Progress was renewed with the revival of commerce in the twelfth century.

The need for lighthouses became more apparent during the seventeenth and eighteenth centuries, after the voyages of exploration made by Columbus (whose uncle Antonio had been the custodian

Opposite: *Point Bonita Light, San Francisco, California.*

of the lighthouse at Genoa), Magellan and others, which greatly increased the distances covered by European vessels sailing into unknown waters. Captains, their crewmen and especially the merchants who financed these voyages wanted some system of warning about the dangers at sea, both at home and abroad. This led to the construction of the most celebrated lighthouse of the modern world, at Eddystone Rock.

Located just 14 miles southwest of the harbor of Plymouth, England, Eddystone Rock is a triple reef 600 yards long. Its twenty-three "rust-red granite rocks" constituted one of the greatest hazards to mariners off the coasts of England and France. Plymouth doubled in size during the seventeenth century, becoming one of the most important ports on the Atlantic (the *Mayflower* sailed from there in 1620), and many ships were lost on the reef, which was difficult to navigate.

Prior to this time, most lighthouses had been built on dry land. It took an audacious engraver and engineer, Henry Winstanley, to attempt the task of building one of the first wave-swept lighthouses. Between 1696 and 1698, Winstanley and his workers, who had to row for six hours just to reach the site, erected an 80-foot-tall lighthouse on the reef. On November 14, 1698, Winstanley lighted several large candles at the top, and all England was surprised and delighted to learn that the treacherous reef had been mastered.

The greatest storm ever recorded in English waters struck the country on the night of November 26, 1703. Citizens, buildings, livestock, ships and sailors were lost throughout the island nation. When dawn came on November 27, only a few pieces of iron and stone were left on the reef: Winstanley and his attendants had been swept away and were never heard from again.

Undaunted, a second builder, John Rudyerd, erected a lighthouse on the same spot between 1706 and 1709. The second lighthouse at Eddystone endured until 1755, when it was destroyed by fire. A third lighthouse began operating in 1759; it remained until 1882, when it was dismantled and brought ashore to Plymouth. The fourth lighthouse, finished in 1882, still stands today. Eddystone Light was depicted on the British penny until 1970—a vivid testimony to the importance of such beacons.

European colonists in North America soon saw the need for aids to coastal navigation in their waters. Boston Light, finished in 1716, was the first. It was followed by the French lighthouses at Louisbourg on Cape Breton Island (1732) and Sambro Island (1758), both in Nova Scotia. Charles Town, South Carolina, finished its lighthouses in 1767, and Cape Ann Light in Massachusetts was completed in 1771. By the time the Declaration of Independence was made in 1776, there were twelve U.S. coastal lighthouses, most of them in New England.

In August 1789, the new United States Congress assumed control of and responsibility for all lighthouses, including those to be built in the future (the first was Portland Head Light, completed in 1791). During the first twenty years of the Republic, Presidents Washington, Adams and Jefferson made all appointments within the lighthouse system personally. The number of beacons grew apace: in 1800 the United States had sixteen; by 1812 the young country boasted no fewer than forty-nine lighthouses.

The manner of lighting had changed by this time. In the ancient world and during medieval times, lighthouses had been illuminated by building large fires, sometimes reflected upward, as was the case at Pharos. During the sixteenth century, large candles were introduced: Henry Winstanley's first tower at Eddystone had displayed the light of eight candles.

In 1781 the Swiss inventor Aimé Argand produced a lamp that had a hollow circular wick. Fueled by fish oil (later vegetable or mineral oil), the Argand lamp equaled the power of seven candles and eliminated the problem of smoky wood or coal fires, which blackened the panes of the towers. In the United States, Captain Winslow Lewis took up the Argand invention and persuaded the federal government to adopt his own lamp and parabolic-reflector system, both patterned after Argand's work. By the time the War of 1812 began, Lewis had outfitted most American lighthouses with his lamps.

Lewis formed a close relationship with Stephen Pleasonton, the Fifth Auditor of the U.S. Treasury. Starting in 1820, the Fifth Auditor became solely responsible for administering American lighthouses, which then numbered seventy. Pleasonton was an able and conscientious bureaucrat—so conscientious, in fact, that he chose to disregard innovative beacon lamps in the belief that Lewis's lamps were the least expensive ones available. As a result, the United States began to lag behind other countries, especially those of Europe.

About 1820 the Frenchman Augustin Fresnel (1788–1827) had invented a new type of lightweight lens: a single light was surrounded by refracting prisms that directed a concentrated beam through a large glass magnifier. This lamp, still called the "Fresnel lens," resembles a beehive in shape. Having concluded that light moves in parabolic rather than longitudinal waves, Fresnel built a lamp that far outshone its rivals. But the American lighthouse system, presided over by Pleasonton, did not deign to install Fresnel lenses for almost two generations!

In 1851 a congressional investigation revealed that American lighthouses were inferior to their foreign counterparts. Pleasonton stepped down, and a

Right: *Scituate Light, Massachusetts;*
Opposite: *Louisbourg Light, Nova Scotia.*

new nine-member Lighthouse Board was created. By this time (1852), the United States had 331 lighthouses and 42 lightships and the closest American equivalent to Eddystone Light was under construction: a wind-and-wave-swept lighthouse off the coast at Cohasset, just south of Boston. The new lighthouse, completed in 1860 at Minots Ledge, was a marvel of design and strategy.

The first Canadian lighthouse was at Fortress Louisbourg on Cape Breton Island, Nova Scotia. Built in 1733, the tower was destroyed in the second British siege of the fortress in 1758. That same year, British-Canadians built Sambro Light in Halifax Harbor.

French Canada passed into British hands in 1763, at which time various boards of commissioners were appointed to manage public works until 1805. Then Québec Trinity House, modeled on the British Trinity House Corporation, was established, followed by the Montreal Trinity House in 1832. These corporations managed lighthouse affairs in eastern Canada, where immigration from Europe via the St. Lawrence River made lighthouses a major consideration.

The Confederation of Canada placed all lighthouses under the Department of the Marine in 1870, when there were 131 lights in present-day Québec and Ontario. From this time, emphasis shifted to the west coast, where the burgeoning province of British Columbia needed protection for Pacific shipping lanes. The Department of the Marine created six regional agencies in 1876, and in 1904 the Canadian Lighthouse Board took charge of all aids to navigation. That responsibility devolved upon the Department of Transport in 1936. When Newfoundland (which remained part of the British Empire) finally entered the Confederation in 1949, its many lighthouses were enrolled in Canada's impressive list of fixed aids to navigation.

The Victorian period represented a golden age in the history of lighthouses. Between 1852, when the Lighthouse Board was created, and 1910, when it was superseded by the Bureau of Lighthouses, the number of aids to navigation in the United States had grown from 331 lighthouses and 42 lightships to 11,713 installations of all kinds, includ-

ing the cannons and bells that had been employed for centuries as adjuncts to the beacons. During this time, the United States built the first West Coast lighthouses, at Alcatraz Island and Point Pinos, Monterey, California, completed in 1854 and 1855, respectively. Another important addition was the lighthouse at Cape Disappointment, near the mouth of the Columbia River. At least 200 ships had been wrecked on or near this ill-starred headland before the light was built.

What about the keepers of the lights? Charles Dickens was

surely mistaken (or ironic) when he declared in *The Pickwick Papers*, "Anythin' for a quiet life, as the man said when he took the situation at the lighthouse." Indeed, it is difficult to conceive how long and laborious the hours were for the lighthouse keepers and their families. Candles had to be lit at night, relit in the early morning hours and extinguished at daylight. Until the late nineteenth century when kerosene was introduced, lanterns were fueled by viscous oils that left a thick, dirty residue on walls and lenses. Living conditions were isolated, damp, drafty and often polluted with mercury and other toxic substances. All of this was merely part of the day-to-day routine: the truly heroic keeper, of whom there are many examples, always kept a sharp lookout for vessels in distress.

The greatest example is Lime Rock Light, built in the harbor of Newport, Rhode Island, in 1854. Hosea Lewis, the first keeper, brought his young family to the island in 1856. He suffered a stroke a year later and became unable to perform his duties, which fell to his oldest child, sixteen-year-old Idawalley Zoradia Lewis, known as "Ida."

Ida Lewis tended the light and rowed her younger siblings to the mainland and back for schooling. Renowned for her strength at rowing and dauntless courage, she saved the lives of four shipwrecked men in 1858, rescued four others in 1866 and prevented two soldiers from drowning in 1869. She was the first woman to receive a Congressional gold medal for lifesaving.

In 1869 *Harper's Weekly* featured a photograph of Ida Lewis on its cover—the very image of feminine strength. That same year, President Ulysses S. Grant visited Lime Rock. When he got his feet wet disembarking from his boat, he declared staunchly: "I have come to see Ida Lewis, and I'd get wet up to my armpits if necessary."

Following the death of her father in 1872, and that of her mother seven years later, Ida Lewis became the official keeper of Lime Rock Lighthouse. She remained in that capacity until her death in 1911. By that time, she had surpassed a half-century of service and had tended Lime Rock Light through 18,250 nights.

Above: *Columbia Lightship, Astoria, Oregon;*
Opposite: *Jupiter Inlet Light, Florida.*

Conical & Cylindrical Lighthouses

 "*As the ultimate stability of a sea-tower, viewed as a monolithic mass, depends,* caeteris paribus, *on the lowness of its centre of gravity, the general notion of its form is that of a cone; but, as the forces to which its several horizontal sections are opposed decrease towards its top in a rapid ratio, the solid should be generated by the revolution of some curve line convex to the axis of the tower, and gradually approaching to parallelism with it.*"

Alan Stevenson, a renowned Scottish engineer, made this summary in his *Rudimentary Treatise on the History, Construction and Illumination of Lighthouses*, published in London in 1850. Stevenson came from the single most distinguished family in the history of lighthouse construction: in three generations, its members built more than eighty towers during the nineteenth and twentieth centuries. It was Alan Stevenson who designed and supervised the building of Skerryvore Light off the coast of Scotland and who articulated the belief that the mass or weight of a tower was more important than its strength. This led to the pre-eminence of conical towers. Eddystone Light, off the coast of Cornwall, had pioneered the use of the conical design, which British and Scottish engineers adopted.

Americans followed the British lead in lighthouse engineering: most of the early beacons of the United States were conical or cylindrical in shape. Made of wood or stone, these early lights had to combine sufficient sturdiness to withstand the waves with the height to be visible at a distance to ships at sea. The primary task of a lighthouse intended to be seen from afar, in terms of height, is to overcome the Earth's arc to project its beam of light. On low-lying coasts, towers must be taller than those on coastal cliffs to achieve the same result.

During the colonial period, when lighthouses were in relatively isolated locations along the coastline, tall towers were necessary. Conical or cylindrical structures, while challenging to build, offered less resistance to wind and waves than would a building with flat planes. Boston Light, first built in 1716, took the form of a conical tower, as did Nantucket Island's Brant Point off the Massachusetts coast. After the Revolutionary War, with the formation of a national government, some of the early colonial lighthouses were rebuilt, while new ones were designed, many as conical stone structures. Maine's Portland Head Light is a primary example of this period.

Built in 1791 at the southern end of Casco Bay, 72-foot Portland Head was designed to guide sailors entering this bay at the southern end of Maine's long coastline. Of course, it was designed to be functional rather than decorative, but Portland Head remains one of the most admired and photographed of all American lighthouses. Just south of it stands Cape Elizabeth Light, a cast-iron tower built in 1874 that shows the durability of the conical form. Similarly, the conical Bass Harbor Head Light, built in 1858, shortly before the Civil War, still stands today.

Like these examples, many New England lighthouses are conical or cylindrical. Cape Cod's Chatham Light was rebuilt in 1877: short and sturdy, this conical white tower was originally one of a pair, until its sister tower was removed to nearby Nauset Beach. Boston Light, which has been built twice, retained its conical tower in the reconstruction of 1783. Connecticut's Stratford Light was a prefabricated, conical, cast-iron tower—the first of its kind in New England.

Ohio's conical Marblehead Light, built by immigrants from New England in 1821 on the Lake Erie shore, resembles the construction style then prevalent on the East Coast. Interestingly, the Marblehead area also produced the granite blocks that would comprise Spectacle Reef Lighthouse on Lake Huron (see chapter 4).

Conical and cylindrical lighthouses were also a common sight in the mid-Atlantic and Southern states. The legendary Cape Hatteras Light (1870), built to replace an earlier tower on the treacherous outer banks of Cape Hatteras, North Carolina, is the nation's tallest and most famous lighthouse. Cape Florida Light was finished in 1825, when the national government was taking more vigorous strides toward uniting the young nation geographically. Biloxi Light on Mississippi's Gulf Coast, finished much later, is an example of the conical cast-iron tower, many of which would follow.

Florida's Ponce de Leon Light is the second tallest of all American lighthouses, exceeded only by Cape Hatteras. It stands as a vivid example of the need for taller lights on the Southern coast, where the land along the sea is lower than it is in New England. This light was erected in 1884–87 to guide mariners along an unlit stretch of coastline that was notorious as a "graveyard." Bolivar Point Light, erected just north of Galveston, Texas, carries poignant memories of the devastating hurricanes that struck Galveston in 1900 and 1915. The lighthouse survived both storms, and all those who took refuge in it were saved.

Unlike the early New England lighthouses, the majority of colonial beacons in Atlantic Canada were octagonal. By the mid-nineteenth century, however, conical towers were gradually replacing these older structures. Particularly well-known are the "Imperial Towers," so named because some were partly funded by the British government. These elegant and distinctive landmarks are tall, white, rugged stone cylinders. Vancouver Island's Race Rocks (1860)—Canada's oldest manned Pacific light—is a fine example of this style; others include Chantry Island Lighthouse, which is one of six Imperial Towers built on Lake Huron between 1855 and 1859.

The first architect for the United States Lighthouse Board had the responsibility of planning the first beacons for the West Coast. The designs his workmen carried out resulted in lights that resembled those on the East Coast to a remarkable degree, including Oregon's Heceta Head and Cape Blanco Lights. The Spanish Revival style in lighthouses would not appear in California until the early twentieth century.

The conical and cylindrical styles that originated in Europe guided the construction of lighthouses during much of North America's development from early colonial days through an era of settlement, population growth and increased economic activity.

Previous pages: *Graves Light, Boston, Massachusetts.*

Portland Head Light
Cape Elizabeth, Maine

Perhaps the most photographed lighthouse in America, Portland Head is also the first to have been built under the auspices of the United States government. In 1787 Massachusetts (which then included Maine) authorized $1,500 for the construction of a lighthouse on Cape Elizabeth. Two years later, the new U.S. Congress set up a "Lighthouse Establishment," through a bill passed on August 7, 1789. President George Washington ordered Secretary of the Treasury Alexander Hamilton to take over the work that had been started by Massachusetts. Congress appropriated $1,500 more to complete the construction.

The work proceeded slowly. Following the president's directions, the builders dragged fieldstone to the site with teams of oxen. By late 1790, the tower—which measured 72 feet from base to lantern—was finished. On January 10, 1791, the first keeper, Joseph Greenleaf, lit sixteen lamps filled with whale oil, and Portland Head shone its light upon the waters off Cape Elizabeth for the first time. Casco

Bay, which extends 20 miles from Cape Elizabeth to Bald Head, has 222 islands; at the time they were called the Calendar Islands, in the mistaken belief that there were 365 of them.

Little changed at Portland Head until 1855, when the Lighthouse Board had the tower lined with brick and installed a metal spiral staircase. A fourth-order Fresnel lens replaced the previous lamps. During the Civil War, Confederate ships sporadically attacked shipping in Portland Harbor. Given the necessity to have Union ships see the light as soon as possible, the tower was raised to 95 feet.

Ten years later, a second-order lens was put into the tower, but the Lighthouse Board reversed itself again in 1883, when the fourth-order lens was reinstalled. The Board made its final decision in 1885, and the second-order lens returned. One year later, the lighthouse witnessed the wreck of the *Anna C. Maguire*, a three-masted bark. Acting with speed and courage, keeper Joshua Strout and his son Joseph saved the lives of the captain, his wife and family, and all fifteen crew members. The Strout family served as keepers of the light for more than three generations. Today, visitors can see this historic lighthouse in Fort Williams State Park.

Cape Elizabeth Light
Cape Elizabeth, Maine

Known as "Two Lights" to locals, the Cape Elizabeth Light uses a second-order Fresnel lens to project a beacon with four million candlepower—the most powerful light of its kind in New England. Located just south of Portland, the station was originally built in 1828, when contractor Jeremiah Barry erected two rubblestone towers 300 yards apart. In 1869 the twin towers received the first steam-driven warning whistles used in the United States. In 1874 both structures were replaced by cast-iron conical towers, each 67 feet high and 129 feet above sea level. The western light was discontinued when the use of multiple lights ended in 1924. The eastern one remains in service. The western tower, sold during the 1970s, now occupies private land, while the eastern tower is next to 41-acre Two Lights State Park.

Despite its beacons, Cape Elizabeth has witnessed many shipwrecks. In January 1885, keeper Marcus A. Hanna made a daring and ingenious rescue of two seamen from the schooner *Australia*, which had run up on Dyers Ledge during a raging snowstorm.

Bass Harbor Head Light
Mount Desert Island, Maine

One of the most picturesque of all American lighthouses, Bass Harbor Head Light stands on a rugged promontory at the eastern entrance to Bass Harbor, which is located at the southwest corner of Mount Desert Island. The 32-foot cylindrical tower was built in 1858 to mark the entrance to Blue Hill Bay and to guide vessels making their way into or out of Bass Harbor. The light is equipped with a fourth-order Fresnel lens, which emits a red flash every four seconds. Not far north of the light is a geological wonder—the only fjord on the East Coast of North America, carved during the last glacial era by ice a mile thick. Somes Sound indents the shoreline to a depth of 7 miles, creating an enclave of natural beauty especially prized by sailors and rock climbers. Mount Desert Island has long been a retreat for artists and writers and a resort for wealthy and prominent Americans including Rockefellers and Astors. The creation of Acadia National Park in 1911 ensured that countless others would be able to enjoy the island as well.

Annisquam Harbor Light

Annisquam, Massachusetts (Opposite)

Marking the east side of the entrance to Annisquam Harbor on Cape Ann, Massachusetts, Annisquam Light (better known as "Squam Light" to the locals) stands on what is called Wigwam Point. It is the oldest of the four lighthouses that have guarded the Gloucester peninsula. The original beacon at Annisquam was built in 1801; it was replaced in 1897 by the 41-foot brick tower that began its service with a fifth-order Fresnel lens. The lens was upgraded in 1972, then replaced by a 190mm plastic optic in 1988. The white light flashes every 7.5 seconds with a red sector. A Coast Guard family lives in the former keeper's house built in 1801. Residents of Annisquam remain proud of their maritime heritage, pointing out that Rudyard Kipling lived there while he wrote *Captains Courageous*, among the greatest literary tributes paid to American sailors.

Chatham Light

Chatham, Massachusetts (Below)

The French explorer Samuel Champlain landed at Stage Harbor in what is now Chatham in 1606. Two centuries later, in 1808, twin wooden towers were built at Chatham Harbor on Cape Cod. The presence of two lights was intended to prevent sailors from mistaking the area for Cape Cod Light, located not far to the north on the same Great Outer Beach. During the 1830s, the towers were dismantled and replaced by brick structures. In 1877 the threat of erosion prompted construction of two cast-iron towers at a safer site. However, because many mariners found the dual lights confusing, the south tower was dismantled in 1923 and moved to **Nauset Beach** (page 28). The conical north tower, which is 48 feet tall, still stands at Chatham.

Stratford Point Light
Stratford, Connecticut

Located at the western side of the mouth of the Housatonic River, on Long Island Sound, the first Stratford Point Light was built in 1822 as a shingled frame tower. The beacon was lit by whale oil, then by lard, and in 1850 the light received a fifth-order Fresnel lens and a bell tower. In 1881 the bell tower was replaced and the present tower built and fitted with a new third-order lens. Thirty-five feet high, with a focal point 52 feet above sea level, this was the first cast-iron conical tower built in Connecticut, and one of the first in the country. During a fierce eight-day snowstorm, the bell tolled for 104 consecutive hours; after a brief lull, it rang for another 103 hours. An air siren replaced the bell in 1911. Today, the lighthouse still guards the mouth of the river, which retains its rural look despite the presence of the nearby Igor Sikorsky Memorial Airport.

West Quoddy Head Light
West Quoddy Head, Maine

West Quoddy Head is a thickly wooded peninsula connected to Lubec, Maine, by a small strip of land. The lighthouse stands on the eastern end of the island. Indeed, despite its name, the light stands at the easternmost point of the United States (longitude 66°, 57' West); its Canadian neighbor **Head Harbour (East Quoddy)** (pages 52–53) accounts for the apparent misnomer. President Thomas Jefferson gave the order for construction, and in 1808 Thomas Dexter lit the first wicks in the lanterns, 90 feet above sea level. Overlooking Quoddy Narrows, which separates the United States from Canada, West Quoddy Light played an important role in aiding mariners stranded in thick banks of fog in the Bay of Fundy, between New Brunswick and Nova Scotia. A 500-pound bell—the first to be used as a fog signal in the United States—was installed in 1820.

The lighthouse was pulled down and reconstructed in 1858. The new tower rose to 85 feet above sea level and was equipped with a third-order Fresnel lens, which displays a pair of two-second flashes four times per minute. The handsome candy-cane stripes on the lighthouse (eight red and seven white) make for easy identification. Standing at the lighthouse, the visitor can look east to Roosevelt Campobello International Park and south to Canada's Grand Manan Island.

Boston Light
Little Brewster Island, Massachusetts *(Opposite)*

Boston Light was built on what is now called Little Brewster Island by the Province of Massachusetts Bay in 1716. It was the first lighthouse in the thirteen colonies, a cone-shaped stone tower, lit first by tallow candles and later by an oil lamp. George Worthylake, the first keeper, served for only two years before his untimely death in a capsized boat. He has been succeeded by more than sixty other keepers, and in 1989 Congress voted to man the light permanently. Today, it is the only American lighthouse with a keeper.

At the beginning of the Revolutionary War in 1775, Boston was the garrison of the British army in North America. Attacked twice by Patriot militiamen, the British destroyed the lighthouse.

After the war, a new tower, 75 feet high, was completed. It has withstood more than 200 years of wind and water. In 1859 a second-order Fresnel lens of 1,800,000 candlepower was installed, whose light is visible 16 miles from shore.

In spite of the caliber of this lighthouse, many ships have come to grief near Little Brewster Island. Scientifically, these losses are still below average, but Boston sailors tell of an area they call the "Ghost Walk," several miles east of the light. They claim that they cannot hear the signal from Boston Light in the Ghost Walk, which remains a haunted region in New England maritime folklore.

Bonilla Island Light
Off Banks Island, Hecate Strait, British Columbia *(Below)*

Bonilla Island Light is a cylindrical white fiberglass tower 32 feet high. Erected in 1960, it was the last lighthouse built on the west coast of Canada. The station is actually located on a smaller island west of Bonilla, to which it is connected at low tide. It is surrounded by ledges and rocks and situated in a scenic archipelago of islands off the fjord-carved coastline near Prince Rupert. Northwest and South Rocks, equidistant from the island, constitute the greatest hazards for mariners.

Bonilla Light identifies the major channels that lead to the busy port of Prince Rupert, one of the world's largest deepwater terminals. Once a Hudson's Bay post, the town has experienced expansion since the increase in trade among the Pacific Rim countries. The tower and station are staffed by two families who make their homes here. Because of their remote location, they receive their supplies by Coast Guard helicopter and are expected to keep two months' worth of necessities on hand at all times.

Cape May Light
Cape May Point, New Jersey

The white tower of Cape May Light rises above a reed-filled marsh. Located on the northern side of Delaware Bay, at the southernmost part of New Jersey, Cape May claims to be the oldest seaside resort in the United States. During the late nineteenth century, the town rivaled Newport, Rhode Island, as a fashionable summer place. Cape May was called the "Resort of Presidents" because Buchanan, Lincoln, Grant, Hayes, Arthur and Harrison all vacationed there. In 1823 a 170-foot tower was built on the western side of Cape May, but it soon fell victim to erosion. The tower was rebuilt in 1847, but it, too, was soon endangered by shifting sands. In 1859 the Lighthouse Board had a new 170-foot white tower with a red lantern built well to the north of the earlier structures. Cape May Light had to be tall because of the low-lying nature of the coast, which is typical of the Atlantic coastal plain from here south. At 165 feet above sea level, Cape May's first-order Fresnel lens emits a light of 600,000 candlepower that still guides ships into Delaware Bay. The lighthouse is on the grounds of Cape May Point State Park, an area well known for its many species of birds and the site of the Audubon Cape May Bird Observatory.

Nauset Beach Light

Eastham, Massachusetts (Opposite)

Well known as the former site of the "Three Sisters of Nauset," the lone light at Nauset Beach today is a conical cast-iron tower 48 feet high. The first "triple set" of lights was built here in 1838, when three cast-iron towers, 150 feet apart, were erected. The nation's only triple light existed in this form until 1892, when the crumbling towers were replaced by three wooden structures placed 30 feet farther inland. In 1911 the number of lights was reduced to one, which lit the area until 1923, when it was replaced by one of the two lights from **Chatham** (page 20). Historic Nauset Beach Light was threatened again by severe land erosion in recent years and was saved by relocation in 1996.

Marblehead Light

Marblehead, Ohio (Below)

Marblehead Light is the oldest active lighthouse on the Great Lakes. Located on the tip of a bow-shaped peninsula that juts out from the southwest corner of Lake Erie, and at the entrance to Sandusky Bay, the light was constructed in 1821. The tower was originally 55 feet tall, but at some point it was raised to 65 feet so that it could accommodate an improved lighting system. The lime-and-white cone-shaped tower houses a fourth-order Fresnel lens and exhibits a flashing green light, which is visible for up to 16 miles. The U.S. Coast Guard still operates the beacon, whose site is now an Ohio State Park.

Race Rocks Light
Strait of Juan de Fuca, British Columbia

The magnificent rusticated-granite Race Rocks Light stands at the eastern end of the Strait of Juan de Fuca, the border between Washington State and British Columbia. Located just south of the important Vancouver Island harbors of Victoria and Esquimalt, Race Rocks was named by a Hudson's Bay Company official in 1842. An 1846 surveyor observed that "This dangerous group is appropriately named, for the tide makes a perfect race around it." Many ships were lost at or near Race Rocks, and in 1859, during the Fraser River gold rush, it was decided to build two lighthouses: one at Fisgard, outside the harbor of Esquimalt, and the other at Race Rocks. They are the oldest lighthouses on the west coast of Canada.

The granite blocks for Race Rocks were cut in Scottish quarries and shipped 16,000 sea miles to Victoria. The station was lighted on Boxing Day (December 26) 1860, only three days after the merchant ship *Nanette* was wrecked on Race Rocks. George Davies was the first keeper of the light. *Nanette* was the last ship to run afoul of Race Rocks on a clear night, but fog remained a persistent danger. Not even the installation of steam and compressed-air horns in 1892 could guarantee safety: the *Prince Victor* was ripped apart in 1901, and the ferry *Sechelt* went down with her crew and all fifty passengers in 1911. The commanding Race Rocks tower endures today as one of the finest examples of Canada's famous "Imperial Lights."

Cape Hatteras Light

Buxton, Outer Banks of Cape Hatteras, North Carolina

The 196-foot black and white tower on the Outer Banks of Cape Hatteras is the tallest on the continent, and the waters around it—the shallow Diamond Shoals—are among the most dangerous. Indeed, this stretch of coastline, legendary as the site of thousands of shipwrecks, is known as the "Graveyard of the Atlantic." The light is located near the site of the 1585 "Lost Colony" of Roanoke, which mysteriously disappeared. Henry Dearborn (1751–1829), a Revolutionary War veteran, congressman and future Secretary of War, built the first beacon here 95 feet above sea level, lighted in 1803. In 1853 the new Lighthouse Board had the tower raised to 150 feet and a first-order Fresnel lens was installed. Early in the Civil War, the Confederate States removed the lens to endanger Federal ships. The light was restored to service in 1862, but the tower itself was soon found to be beyond repair.

Engineer Dexter Stetson erected the present tower at Buxton (1868–70), and in 1873 the lighthouse was painted black and white in the spiral-band pattern that makes it such an effective daymark. However, the travails of the lighthouse were far from over: erosion began to threaten its stability. When Henry Dearborn had erected the first tower, it had been 1,500 feet from the ocean, but by the 1930s, that distance had eroded to some 300 feet. A new skeleton tower was built a mile from the light and the lens installed, while the former site was given over to the National Park Service. Erosion had abated by the early 1950s, and the Coast Guard then agreed with the National Park Service to return the Fresnel lens to the old tower, which served again as a functional aid to navigation. Erosion eventually encroached upon the site once more, however, and in 1999 the light was moved farther inland.

Cape Florida Light
Miami, Florida

One of the few American lighthouses ever to witness armed combat, Cape Florida Light was finished in 1825. Built on the cape at the northern entrance to Biscayne Bay, the original tower was 65 feet tall, made of solid brick, and 5 feet thick at the base. The light guided mariners who passed the dangerous Florida Reef and entered the Cape Florida Channel. In July 1836, during the Seminole War, Keeper John W. Thompson and Aaron Carter, an African-American servant, faced a day-long siege by the Seminole. Carter was killed, while Thompson, though badly wounded, survived the harrowing ordeal. The tower was not fully repaired and reactivated for ten years, and even then, ship captains complained that the light was poor. In 1855 the Lighthouse Board raised the tower so that the focal plane was 100 feet above sea level. The light was also equipped with a second-order Fresnel lens. However, the lighthouse soon faced a new threat. Confederate troops forced it out of operation between 1861 and 1867. In 1878 it was superseded by a new pile lighthouse on nearby Fowey Rocks. The Cape Florida Light continued to function as a daymark, and the Coast Guard relit the station in 1978. Today, the restored tower can be visited in the Bill Baggs Cape Florida State Recreation Area on Key Biscayne, 6 miles north of Fowey Rocks.

Biloxi Light
Biloxi, Mississippi

The best-known of Mississippi's Gulf Coast lighthouses, Biloxi Light serves today as a landmark to drivers as well as ships. The light now stands in the median strip between the lanes of U.S. Highway 90! The 61-foot cast-iron tower was completed in 1848. Over the years, a number of women served as keepers, the best-known of whom was Maria Younghans, who kept the light from 1867 until 1918—a period of fifty-one years. Her daughter went on to serve until 1929. The tower was painted black in 1867. Many people believed this was to mourn the recent death of Abraham Lincoln, but it was actually done so the light would be more visible to mariners. This proved not to be the case, and the tower was repainted white. Biloxi Light is open to the public during the summer.

Bolivar Point Light
Bolivar Point, Texas

Bolivar Point Light is located on Bolivar Peninsula, just north of Galveston Island, Texas. The 117-foot brick-lined iron tower was built in 1873. At that time, Galveston was in the midst of an economic boom and was referred to as the "Queen of the Gulf." But on September 8, 1900, a tremendous hurricane struck the city. When the storms and winds subsided, 6,000 people (some estimates run as high as 8,000) lay dead, and the city was in ruins. But the 125 persons who had found refuge in Bolivar Point Lighthouse were safe. Determined never to be at the mercy of storms again, the people of Galveston built a 17-foot-high, four-mile-long seawall to protect themselves. Finished in 1910, the seawall ensured that Galveston endured much less damage during the next severe hurricane, which came in 1915. Galveston lost 275 citizens in the storm, but the 50 people in the lighthouse were unharmed. The Bureau of Lighthouses discontinued the tower in 1933 and later sold it. Today, the tower is privately owned; the two dwellings next to it are used as summer cottages.

Ponce de Leon Inlet Light
Ponce de Leon Inlet, Florida

Originally known as Mosquito Inlet, and since 1927 as Ponce de Leon Inlet, this body of land lies just south of Daytona Beach, Florida. In 1835 the first lighthouse tower was constructed at Mosquito Inlet, but the oil needed for the lamps did not arrive, and a strong gale washed the sand away from the foundation. Soon afterward, the tower toppled over, a victim of erosion before it ever sent out its first light.

During the 1870s, the Lighthouse Board took notice again of the 60-mile stretch of coast between St. Augustine and Cape Canaveral (now Cape Kennedy) that had no light. Work was begun in 1884, and three years later the present lighthouse stood 168 feet above sea level, making it the second highest of the coastal towers (it is exceeded only by Cape Hatteras at 196 feet above sea level). Equipped with a third-order Fresnel lens, the beacon at Ponce de Leon could be seen up to 19 miles away. In 1970 an aerobeacon at the new Coast Guard station replaced the Ponce de Leon light. Visitors today can climb the recently restored brick conical tower and visit the ancillary buildings.

Heceta Head Light
Florence, Oregon *(Above)*

Heceta Head Light is perched on jagged rocks adjacent to Devil's Elbow State Park, overlooking the Pacific Ocean. Located almost due west of Eugene, Oregon, the 56-foot, conical white masonry tower was built in 1894 to guide ships along the section of coast north of the Siuslaw River. Because lighthouse construction on the Pacific Coast lagged far behind that of its Atlantic counterpart, Heceta Head was the only light between Yaquina Head and Cape Arago, both in Oregon. Equipped with a first-order Fresnel lens whose focal plane is 205 feet above sea level, it casts a light visible 21 miles out to sea.

Cape Blanco Light
Port Orford, Oregon *(Opposite)*

Cape Blanco takes its name from its white cliffs, which were well known to Spanish navigators as early as the seventeenth century. The captains of Spanish treasure galleons came to know Cape Blanco well: they used it as a landmark from which they turned south on their way to Acapulco, Mexico. The waters here are fast and treacherous, and many ships were lost prior to the 1879 construction of the conical masonry tower, only 59 feet tall, but 245 feet above sea level. Its first-order Fresnel lens is measured at one million candlepower. The Lighthouse Board originally called it Cape Orford Light, but the site's Hispanic name had never faded away, and by 1889 it was referred to again as Cape Blanco. Situated at the westernmost point of the Lower Forty-Eight states, historic Cape Blanco is Oregon's oldest operating lighthouse.

Octagonal, Square & Pyramidal Lighthouses

In the United States, octagonal, square and pyramidal light-tower structures became widespread in the years just before the Civil War. As the nation continued to flex its muscles and expand on the Atlantic and Pacific Coasts, as well as the Gulf of Mexico and the Great Lakes, the need for different types of lighthouses became apparent. New coastal cities like San Francisco emerged, and their harbors needed several beacons to guide vessels safely in. In most cases, harbor lights could be shorter than coastal towers, since mariners used them mainly as channel markers, or to identify local hazards. In these relatively protected locations, engineers could use cheaper materials and simpler designs, because the stations were less exposed to storm and wave damage. Other locations, including sheltered sounds, also favored the use of new, more compact beacons.

Economic factors played an important role in these architectural changes. The U.S. economy boomed in the two decades prior to the Civil War. American trading vessels plied the oceans of the world. New Englanders sent granite and ice as far away as India and Sumatra, and American whaling ships ventured as far as the Sea of Japan. Given the increased need for navigational aids, American architects and engineers responded with towers that were more economical and could be constructed more rapidly.

In Canada, octagonal light towers had been the prevailing style since early Colonial times. Wood was favored over stone as a construction material. Although Canada actually has a longer coastline than the United States (the longest of any nation in the world, if one includes her inlets and islands), the challenge in these early days was not so much to direct merchant vessels to a coastal port as to ensure the safety of transport ships bringing immigrants to British North America along the St. Lawrence River. Therefore, most of the lights were built to protect shipping in the harbors of the Maritimes and on the St. Lawrence River itself. Light stations were usually built at an elevation, reducing height requirements for the towers.

The French Lighthouse at Louisbourg (1733) was octagonal, as was the Cape Sambro Light (1758)—the oldest extant lighthouse in Canada today. East Quoddy Light, at the northern tip of Campobello Island, New Brunswick, remains an excellent example of Canada's early octagonal wooden towers. Other examples include Peggy's Cove Light, New Brunswick, and Green Island Light, which stands in Chatham Channel on the coast of British Columbia.

Canadian engineers faced great challenges in building lighthouses on both the Atlantic and Pacific Coasts. A major dilemma on the East Coast was the loss of ships in the Gulf of the St. Lawrence, near its confluence with Cabot Strait between Newfoundland and Cape Breton Island. Bird Rocks Light, built between 1860 and 1870, represents a major victory over the elements in the history of lighthouse construction. Located inland from Cabot Strait, west of Newfoundland and just north of the Magdalen Island, Bird Rocks Island overlooks ships entering the St. Lawrence River and proceeding to the cities of Québec, Montreal, Ottawa and Toronto. Canadian laborers were able to work for only two months of each summer on the island: its 140-foot cliffs are almost perpendicular, and all the equipment and materials had to be hoisted from the water's edge. When it was finally finished in 1870, the 51-foot timber-and-frame tower stood as a symbol of ingenuity and determination.

In the United States, Sandy Hook Light in New Jersey, built in 1764, was the first octagonal tower in the thirteen colonies. The 102-foot tower is still operational today—the nation's oldest working lighthouse. It was preceded only by the Boston Light, originally built in 1716, but destroyed by the British during the Revolutionary War.

On the New England coast, short square towers were built at Wood End, on Cape Cod, and on Derby Wharf, in the harbor of Salem, Massachusetts. The first was erected in 1873; the latter two years earlier. The Derby Wharf Light is an excellent example of the many square structures built to guide smaller craft into tight harbors.

In Rhode Island, Point Judith, at the southeastern point of Narragansett Bay, has an octagonal tower built in 1856, the same year that Beavertail Light was erected on Conanicut Island, in the middle of the bay. In both cases, the more durable octagonal form was probably chosen over the square design to weather the severe storms that threaten the area periodically.

On the Connecticut coast, bordering Long Island Sound, we find New London Harbor and Lynde Point Lights, at the mouths of the Thames and Connecticut Rivers, respectively. Built in 1801, New London Harbor Light essentially retains its original form—a tribute to the strength of octagonal construction. Lynde Point Light is among the most recognizable in southern New England: in fact, a specialty Connecticut license plate commemorates both Lynde Point and the Saybrook Breakwater Light.

In the northern part of the Great Lakes region, ice often poses as great a hazard to lighthouses as waves do in coastal localities. Split Rock Light, on Lake Superior (1911), was built high on a cliff above the water—and the treacherous winter ice—to guide commercial shipping on this great inland waterway. Since its construction, Split Rock Light has remained an emblem of ingenuity in lighthouse building equal to that of Canada's Bird Rocks.

West Coast exemplars include Point Wilson Light in Port Townsend, Washington, and Alki Point Light in Seattle. Conical towers had been chosen for the Pacific Coast sites, including Cape Disappointment at the mouth of the Columbia River, but octagonal and square structures prevailed in the narrower, less exposed waters of Puget Sound. South of here, on Cape Cabrillo at Mendocino, California, we find the Cape-Cod-dwelling type of lighthouse that became popular largely because the chief engineer of the Lighthouse Board during the 1850s favored that style of construction.

As new lighthouse designs came into use with the growth of maritime commerce, they marked expansion from its early footholds on the continent to the farthest reaches of national hegemony.

Previous pages: *Plymouth (Gurnet) Light, Massachusetts.*

Wood End Light
Provincetown, Massachusetts

Wood End Light stands on the south elbow of the curving arm of Cape Cod, just west of Provincetown and north of Long Point Light, where Cape Cod's land area finally drops off into the sea. The white pyramidal tower was built in 1873 and stands 39 feet tall, with the focal plane of its lens at 45 feet above sea level. Originally, the tower was painted brown and had a red flashing light; a fog bell in a second tower was added in 1902. The area has seen many shipwrecks over the years. One of the worst was the collision of a Navy submarine and a Coast Guard cutter in 1927, a disaster in which forty-two men died. Wood End Light was automated in 1961 and the fifth-order lens removed. The light was converted to solar power in 1981. Physically, the lighthouse is identical to Long Point Light, which stands one mile away, at the end of Cape Cod.

Derby Wharf Light

Salem, Massachusetts

Derby Wharf and its eponymous light (both in Salem) are named for Elias Haskett Derby, a local merchant who became the first millionaire in the United States. During the heyday of the Derby fortunes, ships from Salem dominated the East India trade. Even as Salem declined in importance as a port during the mid-nineteenth century, its people wanted to honor their maritime heritage and the name of their former leading citizen. In 1871 Derby Wharf Light was erected at the end of the nearly one-half-mile-long wharf in Salem Harbor. The tower was 12 feet square and 25 feet tall. Lacking quarters for a keeper, the beacon was tended by a lighter. The original tower was red, but it was painted white in 1922. The Coast Guard decommissioned the light in 1977 and transferred the property to the National Park Service. Volunteers worked to restore the building, and in 1983 the station was relit by the Coast Guard. The tower's flashing red signal is now powered by a solar panel and batteries.

Bete Grise Light

Bete Grise, Michigan (Above)

Typical of the changing styles that were employed on the Great Lakes is this compact square tower that is built into a two-story dwelling. Bete Grise Light was built in 1895 in a relatively sheltered location on the Mendota Ship Canal that links Lac La Belle with Lake Superior. This charming yellow-painted light station is now privately owned.

Beavertail Light

Jamestown, Rhode Island (Opposite)

Built in 1749, the first lighthouse tower on the southern tip of Conanicut Island was a 58-foot wooden structure designed by architect Peter Harrison (1716–75) to guide ships passing the island on their way into Narragansett Bay. The tower burned in 1753 and was replaced by a 64-foot rubblestone beacon. Before the American Revolution, Newport, Rhode Island, was a major colonial port. British soldiers targeted the lighthouse and burned it in 1779 as they retreated from the bay, but Rhode Island had the tower repaired and put back into service until 1851, when it was reported as being in poor condition. A new 52-foot square granite tower was built in 1857. Its fourth-order lens, installed in an 1897 upgrade, remained in service until 1991, when it was placed in the nearby Beavertail Lighthouse Museum.

Watch Hill Light

Westerly, Rhode Island

Watch Hill Light stands on a peninsula jutting into Long Island Sound from the area that marks the southern border between Connecticut and Rhode Island. Located in the latter state, the tower is made of granite and measures 10 feet square by 45 feet high. The fourth-order Fresnel lens has its focal plane 61 feet above sea level. As early as colonial times, settlers recognized the need for a signal at this point: a watchtower was built in 1744, but was wiped out by a gale in 1781. The first true light tower on the peninsula was built in 1807. A cylindrical wooden structure, it stood 73 feet above sea level and was first lit by ten whale-oil lamps. The Lighthouse Board had the old tower taken down in 1856 and replaced it with the current tower, which bears a striking resemblance to **Beavertail Light** (pages 44–45), built in the same year. The Coast Guard automated the light and foghorn in 1986, but decommissioned the station a year later. The Watch Hill Improvement Society has restored the former keeper's house as a maritime museum.

Point Judith Light
Narragansett, Rhode Island

Point Judith Light marks both the west side of the entrance to Narragansett Bay and the north side of the eastern entrance to Block Island Sound. The dangerous waters around Point Judith are another "Graveyard of the Atlantic." The first 35-foot tower here was built in 1810. Five years later, it was destroyed during a great hurricane. In 1816 the light was replaced by a 35-foot stone tower, which had a revolving light comprising ten lamps. This tower was itself replaced in 1856 by the present octagonal granite tower, 51 feet high, with the focal plane of its lens 65 feet above sea level. The Lighthouse Board had the upper half of the tower painted brown and the lower half white, to make the structure a more effective daymark. In 1871 ship captains asked that the fog signal be changed from a horn to a whistle: the latter could be heard more distinctly over the surf, and it served to distinguish Point Judith from **Beavertail Light's** siren (pages 44–45). The confluence of Narragansett Bay and Block Island Sound remained busy: in 1907 more than 22,600 vessels passed the lighthouse during daylight hours. Even with the additional safety factor conferred by the light, the waters around Point Judith have remained the scene of numerous shipwrecks. The *Normandy* (1864), *American Eagle* (1870), *Acusionet* (1870), *Venus* (1877), *Cucktoo* (1882), and *Harry A. Barry* (1888) are among the ships that came to grief in these cold waters. Point Judith was automated in 1954.

Lynde Point Light
Old Saybrook, Connecticut

Lynde Point Light stands as a vivid symbol of Connecticut's sea-faring heritage. Dutch mariners located the mouth of the Connecticut River, in the Long Island Sound, early in the seventeenth century, but a sandbar prevented easy access to the waterway. The first tower was built in 1802, on land that had been purchased from William Lynde. Made of wood, the 35-foot tower was often obscured by mist and fog. After numerous complaints from local mariners, the lighthouse that stands today was built in 1838. The 65-foot octagonal stone tower stands guard on the western side of the mouth of the Connecticut River—perhaps the only major river in North America without a city at its entry to the sea. It is flanked instead by two villages: Old Saybrook on the western side, and Old Lyme on the east. A fog bell was added in 1854. The lighthouse was refurbished in 1868, at which time the handsome wooden spiral staircase was added. The light employs a fifth-order Fresnel lens, one of only two Fresnel lenses still in use in Connecticut. Lynde Point displays a fixed white light. After the **Saybrook Breakwater Light** (page 89) was built in 1886, Lynde Point became known as the "Inner Light."

New London Harbor Light
New London, Connecticut

At the western side of the mouth of the Thames River, the New London Harbor Light was the fourth lighthouse built during the American colonial period. Seeing the need for a beacon here, the citizens of New London started a lottery, which, combined with a tax on shipping, paid the building costs. Finished in 1760, the original light was an octagonal stone tower 64 feet high and 24 feet in diameter at the base. The tower survived the Revolutionary War intact, but major repairs soon became necessary, and in 1801 a new 80-foot tower with a focal plane of 111 feet was built at a cost of $15,547. Whale-oil lamps provided the initial light: later, the tower was converted to house a fourth-order Fresnel lens (one of only two still operating in Connecticut today). Much admired for its beauty, the tower was criticized by some of those most concerned—the sailors, who said that it offered inadequate protection from central shoals at the river's mouth. **New London Ledge Light** (page 87) was built to remedy the situation.

Peggy's Cove Light
St. Margaret's Bay, Nova Scotia

The most photographed and perhaps the best-loved light station in Canada, the beautiful Peggy's Cove is a magnet for visitors, artists and marine photographers alike. The charming village of about sixty residents lies just northeast of Peggy's Point, at the eastern entrance to St. Margaret's Bay. Built in 1868, the lighthouse is a white octagonal masonry tower. Only 37 feet high, the picturesque tower is topped by a red metal lantern.

Immense granite ledges mark the area of Peggy's Cove. They are legacies of the last Ice Age, when retreating glaciers deposited the boulders, estimated to be some 400 million years old. The land slopes from the lighthouse to the open Atlantic, forming an inviting area for walking. There is a spectacular stone carving on one granite boulder by the late William E. DeGarthe, who was a resident of Peggy's Cove. It depicts 32 fishermen, their wives and children, a guardian angel, and the legendary Peggy—a fitting tribute to the rugged nature of life in the Canadian Maritimes. The area was the scene of a tragic airline crash in September 1998.

Peggy's Cove is the only lighthouse in North America that doubles as a post office. When a letter is sent from the cove, a unique lighthouse postmark is imprinted over the stamp.

Green Island Light
Chatham Sound, British Columbia

Green Island Light is located 25 miles west of the dramatic fjord-
and mountain-carved coastline of Port Simpson and just 10
miles from the border that separates British Columbia and Alaska.
The first tower was built on this site in 1906; the present tower, built
in 1956, is 30 feet high and has its focal plane 60 feet above sea level.
The light has a range of 13 nautical miles. The octagonal white
masonry tower is detailed in red to serve as a daymark. The *Taku*
ferry between Prince Rupert, British Columbia, and the "salmon
capital," timber and tourist town of Ketchikan, Alaska, passes the
isolated but strategically located Green Island.

Head Harbour (East Quoddy) Light
Campobello Island, New Brunswick

Americans call it East Quoddy Light, but Canadians know this impressive landmark as Head Harbour Light. Standing 45 feet above sea level, the red-and-white octagonal light is located just off the northern tip of Campobello Island in Passamaquoddy Bay, which marks the international boundary between Canada and the United States. Campobello Island is best known as the location of the thirty-four-room summer home of the future U.S. president Franklin D. Roosevelt, who had spent childhood summers there and loved the rugged beauty of this remote retreat. Roosevelt was vacationing there with his wife, Eleanor, and their children when he was stricken with polio in August 1921.

Campobello Island is linked to Lubec, Maine, by the Roosevelt Memorial Bridge. The Roosevelt Campobello International Park, which was established on the island in 1964, is administered by a joint U.S.– Canadian commission.

The Head Harbour Light station was established in 1829. The need for the light became apparent when illegal commerce flourished between the United States and Canada during the period of the Napoleonic Wars, at the start of the nineteenth century. On the American side, at

the eastern extremity of the United States, **West Quoddy Head Light** (page 23) was established in 1808. New Brunswick had only a single light before the nineteenth century, at St. John Harbour, built in 1791. Head Harbour Light, the second, was followed by Gannet Rock, Point Lepreau, Machias, Seal Island and Quaco.

The octagonal tower at Head Harbour is a white wooden, shingle-clad structure, some 45 feet high and 21 feet in circumference at the base. Built of heavy timber, it has been reshingled and repainted many times, but it still appears much as it did originally. The only major change occurred in 1887, when the original lantern was replaced by a new one made of cast iron. The distinctive daymark—a large red cross—has been on the tower at least since the time of Canadian Confederation in 1867. Head Harbour Light is now fully automated, and there is no keeper in residence.

The light and its ancillary buildings occupy all of the barren, rocky point upon which they are located. The point and light station are accessible from Campobello Island for only two hours each day at the low tides. Coming in from the Bay of Fundy, the tides rise at the remarkable rate of 5 feet per hour, and many keepers, as well as tourists, have found themselves stranded on the point. Despite its remote location, Head Harbour Light is a popular destination for summer tourists.

Alki Point Light
Seattle, Washington (Above)

Alki Point Light stands at the southern entrance to Seattle's Elliott Bay in Puget Sound. This is believed to be the site where, in 1851, the schooner *Exact* disembarked the first group of American settlers (12 adults and 12 children) for what would later become the Northwest's Queen City. The point was named for a local chief who befriended the settlers, as the city was named for Chief Seathl of several Puget Sound tribes, who ceded land here in 1855. The light is now located between a single-family house and a low-rise apartment complex. The Coast Guard has posted a *No Trespassing* sign.

Point Wilson Light
Fort Worden, Port Townsend, Washington (Opposite)

Point Wilson Light is located at historic Fort Worden, just outside of Washington State's Port Townsend. The first light here was finished in 1879—a 46-foot wooden tower that gave off a fixed white light with a red flash every 20 seconds. Point Wilson marks the separation between Admiralty Inlet and the extensive Strait of Juan de Fuca, and Port Townsend boomed during the 1890s because there was reason to hope that the town might become the terminus for an important railroad line. Those hopes were dashed when railroad management selected Seattle instead. Point Wilson received a new tower, 51 feet above sea level in 1913–14, on the eve of World War I. The picturesque Port Townsend, with its quaint Victorian houses, has remained a busy logging and ferry port that serves Vancouver Island, and the octagonal concrete tower is still active. Moviegoers may recall the area and scene from the popular film *An Officer and a Gentleman.*

Split Rock Light
Two Harbors, Minnesota

"The unusual local magnetic attractions and the impossibility of getting reliable soundings in the neighborhood make navigation difficult in thick weather." This was a salient point in the report produced by the Lighthouse Board in an effort to have a beacon built on this site on the shores of Lake Superior.

Located northeast of Duluth and twenty miles north of Two Harbors, Minnesota, Split Rock Light offers one of the most breathtaking sights to be found on the Great Lakes. The imposing 54-foot octagonal brick light tower stands high on a rock that juts out into Lake Superior. Its third-order Fresnel lens used incandescent oil-lamp lighting to produce the station's 1.2 million candlepower.

The need for a lighthouse at this site was made clear by the wrecks of many ore carriers on Lake Superior at the turn of the twentieth century. The Lighthouse Board selected the promontory, which rises 130 feet above the edge of the lake. Construction began in May 1909. Although the work proceeded rapidly, it was far from easy: a derrick was used to lift hundreds of tons of building material up to the promontory from the decks of lakegoing vessels.

Three two-story keepers' dwellings, storage buildings, a fog signal building and an oil house were also completed. In August 1910, the third-order bivalve lens (which resembles a clamshell rather than a beehive in shape) was lighted for the first time. The Coast Guard decommissioned the light in 1969. The state of Minnesota took possession of the beacon and grounds in 1970 and created a 2,500-acre park, of which the historic station is the centerpiece.

Point Cabrillo Light
Mendocino, California (Opposite)

L ocated 130 miles north of San Francisco, at the mouth of the Big River, Point Cabrillo was discovered by Juan Rodriguez Cabrillo in 1542. However, the area did not become widely settled by non-Native people until the time of the California Gold Rush, and then only by chance. In 1850 the brig *Frolic*, carrying goods from China, was wrecked off Cape Cabrillo en route to San Francisco. Two years later, salvagers stumbled upon groves of gigantic redwood trees inland from the cape. The area soon became the center of the state's north-coast lumber industry; many came from the East Coast and built towns that gave the region a New England look.

Built in 1909, Point Cabrillo Light is only 47 feet high. However, the tower stands on a site 422 feet above sea level, making it the highest in the United States. The light and fog signal served as an important beacon for lumber schooners sailing off the coast of northern California. After the lumber trade declined, the population of Mendocino dwindled, and today, the entire town has been declared an historic area.

Cape Meares Lighthouse
Tillamook, Oregon (Below)

T his 38-foot octagonal brick tower, clad in sheet iron, was planned for nearby Cape Lookout, but erected in 1889 on this cliff site due to a mapmaker's error. Nevertheless, the station, which stands 217 feet above sea level, guided shipping along the Oregon coast with its first-order Fresnel lens from 1890 until 1963, when it was deactivated by the Coast Guard. It has been restored and is now part of Cape Meares State Park.

Eclectic & Victorian Lighthouses

everal eclectic styles in lighthouse building flourished from pre-Civil War days until the early twentieth century. Like their colleagues in architecture, some engineers focused on building foursquare functional structures more notable for durability than for grace. Others were influenced by popular styles, including revivals of the traditional Nantucket, Cape Cod, New England farmhouse and other vernacular forms. These succeeded one another rapidly as Americans became more prosperous during the Victorian era, and experimented more widely with design and decoration.

Many of the nineteenth-century lighthouses were sited on land that was far enough from the water to reduce the hazards of wind-driven waves. They often took the form of a short tower on the roof of the keeper's dwelling, or attached to it. Both of the beacons at Block Island, for example, were rebuilt after the Civil War. The North Light (1867) became a sturdy granite house with the light tower at one end of the gable roof. The new Southeast Light (1873) crowned a red-brick residence in the popular Gothic Revival Style.

Farther south in New England, several Connecticut lighthouses show period influence. The second beacon at Stonington Harbor, built in the 1840s, was a severely simple masonry cottage with a 35-foot conical tower attached. Replaced in service by the Stonington Breakwater Light in 1889, the property is now a maritime museum owned by the Stonington Historical Society.

Noank's Morgan Point Light, rebuilt in 1867–68, is a handsome three-story building of New England granite with the former light tower centered over the front entrance at the peak of the slate roof. Its gable ornamentation reflects the decorative Eastlake style and marks Noank's transition from a simple fishing village to a modest maritime resort, with many historic period buildings. The former lighthouse is now on private property.

The mid-Atlantic state of New Jersey was one of America's first seaside resorts, and its coastline is dotted with historic lighthouses in several different styles. In Navesink, the original Twin Lights marking the western entrance to New York Harbor were replaced by an imposing stone fortification in the Romanesque style. North Wildwood's picturesque Hereford Inlet Lighthouse was built in the fashionable Stick style, with a square light tower rising from the keeper's house to a height of 57 feet. At Sea Girt, on the Jersey Shore, a rambling Victorian brick structure with a square tower at the intersection of the L-shaped wings rose in 1896 and remained in service until 1945, when the Coast Guard turned it over to the town.

In the Midwest, a stately 110-foot light tower surrounded by impressive buildings congruent with the wealthy Chicago suburb of Evanston was built on Lake Michigan's Grosse Point. The station included an Italianate double keeper's dwelling of yellow brick with hipped and gabled roofs and several brick barns used for fog-signaling equipment. Designed as the primary coastal light on Lake Michigan, Grosse Point was automated in 1935 and eventually turned over to the city of Evanston, which maintains the property and its attractive grounds.

On the Northwest Coast, Oregon's Coquille River Lighthouse (1896) was built of stucco-covered brick with a double keeper's dwelling, a barn and a low fog-signal building attached to the tower. This complex north of Cape Blanco guided ships entering the Coquille River until 1939 and has been partially restored by the state of Oregon as part of scenic Bullards Beach State Park. Adjacent Washington State saw construction of the picturesque Mukileto Lighthouse—an octagonal 30-foot tower with a dwelling and ancillary buildings in a modified Greek Revival Style—in 1906. Seattle's West Point Lighthouse rose on the east side of Puget Sound in 1881. A 23-foot stucco tower supported by a symmetrical house with a multilevel roofline, this landmark is now at risk because of logs and other debris thrown up from the sound. Farther south, in Crescent City, California, a Cape Cod-style dwelling with a short roof-centered tower (1856) shows the typical form of early West Coast lighthouses on Battery Point.

On Liberty Island (formerly Bedloe's Island) in New York City's harbor stands the monumental sculpture that, unknown to many, once served as a lighthouse. Its creator, Frenchman Frédéric-Auguste Bartholdi, entitled it *Liberty Enlightening the World*. Commissioned as a gift from the French people to the American people, it was presented to the United States on July 4, 1884, and installed in the harbor at a cost of $400,000. The sculptor's inspiration for the image was his own mother and Eugène Delacroix's 1830 painting *Liberty Leading the People to the Barricades*.

Parisian engineer Alexandre Gustave Eiffel, the designer of the Eiffel Tower, engineered the internal framework of iron and steel, and the American architect Richard Morris Hunt designed the 154-foot-high pedestal, which was constructed of Stony Creek granite and concrete. Funds for the pedestal were raised by public subscription. The statue itself stands 151 feet tall, with the right arm upholding the beacon and the left clasping a tablet that is inscribed with the date of the Declaration of Independence.

Dedicated by President Grover Cleveland on October 28, 1886, the Statue of Liberty stood on foundations built by Francis Hopkinson Smith, cobuilder of the Race Rock Light in Fishers Island Sound. Within weeks of the dedication, President Cleveland directed the secretary of the treasury to put the Statue of Liberty under the auspices of the Lighthouse Board. It became operational as an aid to navigation on November 22, 1886, when nine arc lamps shone from the torch. The light could be seen from 24 miles out at sea. However, the monument's use as a lighthouse posed serious financial problems. It cost $10,000 per year to keep the beacon lit, and the Statue of Liberty was discontinued as an aid to navigation on March 1, 1902.

In her poem "The New Colossus" (1883), Emma Lazarus compared the Statue of Liberty to the great Colossus of Rhodes, which may have served as a lighthouse when it was one of the Seven Wonders of the ancient world.

Previous pages: *Block Island North Light, Rhode Island.*

Block Island North Light
Block Island, Rhode Island (Opposite)

Lying directly south of mainland Rhode Island at the entrance to Long Island Sound, scenic Block Island is 6 miles long. The waters off the island are well known to be hazardous due to shoals, sandbars, fog and swift currents: even small craft allow for a half-mile clearance while rounding the island. Between 1819 and 1838, fifty-nine different vessels (two full-rigged ships, eight brigs, thirty-four schooners and fifteen sloops) came to grief in these waters. During the late 1820s, the first lighthouse was built at the northern tip of Block Island to warn sailors away from Sandy Point, a sandbar that extends several miles north from the island. This beacon displayed two lights at opposite ends of a single building. However, the lighthouse would serve for less than a decade: the dual lights were sometimes confusing to sailors, and the building itself soon became threatened by erosion.

In 1837 the second Sandy Point Light was built a quarter-mile farther inland: it, too, had two lights mounted on a single building. This time sailors complained that when they were 3 miles away from the Point, the lights blurred into one. In 1857 a third structure was built, but it was soon overcome by the shifting of large masses of sand. It seemed impossible to "get this one right."

The fourth and final lighthouse on Sandy Point, located at the end of Cow Neck Road, was built in 1867. Eight years later, when the **Southeast Light** (page 69) was built, Sandy Point Light was renamed Block Island North Light. The granite structure, which has an iron tower on the roof of the three-story dwelling, contained a fourth-order Fresnel lens that displayed a single fixed white light visible for more than 13 miles. (Later, the signal was changed to a flashing white light.) Henry Ball, who kept the light for many years, was appointed by Abraham Lincoln.

The most horrific maritime accident in Block Island's history occurred on the night of February 11, 1907, when the schooner *Henry Knowlton* collided head-on with the passenger steamer *Larchmont*, which was bound for New York City. Only nineteen passengers from the *Larchmont* survived; the captain and six crew members of the *Henry Knowlton* rowed to the Rhode Island shore. Some 150 persons perished in the tragedy.

Block Island North Light was electrified during the 1940s and automated in 1955. The U.S. Fish and Wildlife Service purchased the light and the surrounding 28 acres when the lighthouse was deactivated in 1973. The area soon became a wildlife refuge that sheltered many species of birds. In 1984 the Fish and Wildlife Service sold the structure and the land to the town of New Shoreham for the token price of $1.00. A $400,000 federal grant for restoration was made in 1989, and the lighthouse was relit late that year. Today, the restored first floor of the lighthouse—which is known to locals as "Old Granitesides"—serves as a museum.

Stonington Harbor Light
Stonington, Connecticut

The compact granite lighthouse at Stonington was built on Windmill Point in 1824. It was the first in Connecticut to be constructed by the federal government, rather than by the state government using federal funds. After erosion threatened the site, the lighthouse was torn down and relocated in 1840 to the east side of the harbor. The 35-foot tower was attached to a stone dwelling. In 1889 the light was decommissioned when the Stonington Breakwater Light was built farther out in the harbor. The Stonington Historical Society took custody of the former light for use as The Old Lighthouse Museum. Its sixth-order Fresnel lens is one of the most significant of the society's acquisitions. Stonington has a long and distinguished nautical history: one of its sons was Captain Nathaniel Palmer, who discovered what is now called Palmer Land on a voyage to Antarctica in 1820.

Sheffield Island Light
Norwalk, Connecticut

The site of this historic lighthouse, once called Smith Island, commands the west entrance to the Norwalk River on northern Long Island Sound. The island was deeded to Norwalk's first minister, Thomas Hanford, by Winnipauk, chief of a local tribe, in 1690. By 1826 the island had been owned by the Smith family for five generations, and the first lighthouse here was built on land purchased from the Smiths by the U.S. government. The 30-foot tower was tended by a series of keepers until 1868, when the picturesque Victorian dwelling, with its light tower at the gable end, was erected. In its masonry construction, it resembled nearly all of the major lights built before 1870, when iron replaced stone as the primary structural material. Its fourth-order Fresnel lens emitted a fixed white light varied by red flashes, visible for more than 12 miles. Several similar lighthouses were constructed on Long Island Sound at this time, including those at Port Jefferson, on Long Island, and Great Captain Island, in Greenwich, Connecticut. Sheffield Island Light was deactivated in 1900 when Greens Ledge Light was built a little farther west. In 1987 the Norwalk Seaport Association purchased the 118-year-old lighthouse for renovation and restoration.

Navesink Twin Lights
Highlands, New Jersey

Located on the Atlantic Highlands, the twin lights at Navesink are almost due south of Sandy Hook, New Jersey. Two rubblestone octagonal towers were built there in 1828, to mark the western entrance to New York Bay. In 1840 the towers received the first Fresnel lenses installed in any American lighthouse: Commodore Matthew C. Perry (who later opened Japan to trade with the United States) imported the lenses from France. By the time the Lighthouse Board was established in 1852, it had become obvious that the Fresnel was far superior to any earlier type of lens, and what had begun at Navesink was soon implemented across the country. When the original towers showed considerable signs of wear, they were replaced in 1862 by two new brownstone towers—octagonal and square—connected by a brownstone dwelling. Each was fitted with a first-order Fresnel lens with its focal plane 246 feet above sea level. In 1883 the innovative lights at Navesink became the first in the nation to use mineral oil; and in 1898 the south tower received the first electric arc bivalve lens, and its twin was taken out of service. The light was automated in 1949 and decommissioned by the Coast Guard in 1953. Today, the state of New Jersey owns the site, where it has created a lighthouse museum.

Block Island Southeast Light
Block Island, Rhode Island

In 1875 President Ulysses S. Grant signed an appropriation for the construction of a lighthouse on the southeast side of Block Island. Grant was no stranger to lighthouses or to Rhode Island: he had previously visited Ida Lewis, the famous keeper of Lime Rock Light in Newport. Built 300 feet from the drop-off of the Mohegan Bluffs into the ocean, Southeast Light was constructed in the Victorian Gothic style. The project cost $80,000, including $10,000 for the first-order Fresnel lens. At 52 feet high and 258 feet above sea level, this was the highest light in all New England. The station was electrified in 1928. During the disastrous hurricane of 1938, the lighthouse lost its power, and the keepers had to turn the lens by hand for several days. The Mohegan Bluffs have suffered continuous erosion, and in 1993 the tower was moved to its present location, 300 feet from the new drop-off. Block Island Southeast Light was relighted in August 1994. It is one of the most important stations in New England, as it signals sailors coming from the Atlantic into the waters of Block Island and Long Island Sounds.

Hereford Inlet Light

North Wildwood, New Jersey (Opposite)

This picturesque beacon, built in 1874, rises from a Stick-style dwelling that overlooks the wide inlet leading from the Atlantic to the Intra-Coastal Waterway at North Wildwood, once a small fishing village known as Anglesea. The 50-foot tower and its beacon are visible for up to 13 nautical miles. In 1913 a severe storm damaged the foundation of the lighthouse, and it was moved 150 feet to the west to provide it with a more secure footing. The station was decommissioned in 1964, when an automatic light tower was built. Today, Hereford Inlet Light is owned by the town of North Wildwood.

Sea Girt Light

Sea Girt, New Jersey (Below)

Located due south of Asbury Park, this two-story L-shaped brick building was built in 1896. The light tower rises from the intersection of the wings. In 1921 the first radio fog beacon was installed at Sea Girt, as a navigational aid to ships as they approached New York Harbor. By the 1930s, the inlet around the light had become very shallow, and in 1945 the Coast Guard decommissioned the light and turned the property over to the small town of Sea Girt. In 1981 the Sea Girt Citizens Committee began to restore the lighthouse for use as a civic building.

Crescent City Light
Crescent City, California

Crescent City residents call their municipality the place "where the redwoods meet the sea." Located close to the border with Oregon, Crescent City Light is on the seaward side of a small islet off Battery Point: visitors can reach the structure only at low tide. The Cape Cod-style white-painted stone dwelling with a brick tower attached was among the first group of sixteen lighthouses to be built on the U.S. West Coast and was finished in 1856. The red lantern at the top was given a fourth-order Fresnel lens and emitted a fixed light that was interrupted every 90 seconds by a white flash. In 1907 the original lens was replaced by a new fourth-order lens, which had four panels of glass separated by one of metal. This new lens produced an even more distinctive flash. In 1953 the Coast Guard automated the light and leased the property to the Del Norte County Historical Society, which keeps the light open to the public. The society relit the light, which is now a private aid to navigation, under the title of Battery Point Light Museum.

Just off the coast from Crescent City stands another historic West Coast beacon: St. George Reef Lighthouse, one of the most expensive ever to be built in the United States because of its exposed site. Unfortunately, it has now fallen into disrepair. The St. George Reef (which was once known as Dragon Rock) claimed many ships over the years: the most disastrous wreck occurred in July 1865, when the sidewheeler USS *Brother Jonathan* went down with a loss of 215 lives. In 1882 the Lighthouse Board had the reef and rocks surveyed, and between 1887 and 1892, a square granite light tower was built on top of reinforced concrete, which itself stood on an elliptical base of granite. Built at an elevation of 144 feet above sea level, the light cost $704,000—the most expensive installation to that time. It was originally manned by a crew of four men, but their extreme isolation and the difficulties and inherent dangers of supplying them led the Coast Guard to close the lighthouse in 1975. A large navigational buoy was placed near the reef. During the 1850s, Crescent City was the busiest lumbering port on the Pacific Coast, and these two lighthouses helped keep commerce thriving. The town once supplied lumber to build the burgeoning city of San Francisco.

Grosse Point Light
Evanston, Illinois

The Lighthouse Board ordered construction of a lighthouse at Grosse Point in 1873, after Evanston citizens complained that ships might founder on the shoals off the point. Located just north of Chicago, Evanston is on Lake Michigan. Its 110-foot tower, made of brick now encased in concrete, was equipped with a second-order lens having a focal plane 121 feet above lake level. The fixed white light emitted a red flash every three minutes and was connected to the keeper's building by an enclosed brick passageway. The light was automated by the Bureau of Lighthouses in 1935 and decommissioned by the Coast Guard in 1941. After World War II, it was restored and relighted by private interests as a local aid to navigation. Today, the Evanston Environmental Association runs programs at the Lighthouse Nature Center, and the grounds are part of the 10-acre Lighthouse Landing Park.

Coquille River Light
Bandon, Oregon

Coquille River Light is located at the mouth of the river in Bandon, Oregon, which lies north of **Cape Blanco** (page 36) and Coos Bay. The region was originally home to the Coquille Indians, who found it overrun by American migrants at the start of the California Gold Rush. Today, the small coastal village of Bandon calls itself the "Cranberry Capital of Oregon." The light was built in 1896 above a walking beach with weathered monoliths. The 40-foot conical brick tower stands 47 feet above sea level; a fog-signal building was attached to the tower. The station also has a one-and-a-half-story double keepers' dwelling and a barn. The light was discontinued in 1939 and eventually fell into serious disrepair. It had been vandalized and was in ruinous condition when the Army Corps of Engineers acquired the property in 1960: the barn and dwelling were no longer standing. The State of Oregon leased the property from the Corps of Engineers and made the restored lighthouse part of Bullard Beach State Park. It is believed that the park area was the site of a massacre in 1854, when seventeen members of a non-local tribe were murdered by a group of forty miners.

West Point Light

Seattle, Washington (Above)

West Point Light stands at the end of a peninsula on the east side of Puget Sound, at the point where ships turn to head into the port of Seattle. The 23-foot square brick tower is covered with stucco and is located close to the water's edge. The fourth-order Fresnel lens is 27 feet above sea level. The rest of the station is made up of two frame keepers' dwellings, an oil house and a fog-signal building. The Coast Guard has piled heavy stone at the base of the tower to ward off debris, particularly logs, which wash up from the waters of the Sound. Today, the lighthouse is part of Discovery Park.

Mukileto Light

Mukileto, Washington (Opposite)

Mukileto Light is located just south of Everett, Washington, near the ferry that takes both commuters and tourists to scenic Whidbey Island in Puget Sound. Built in 1906, the light was designed to guide ships through Possession Sound and on to Everett, an important lumber and railroad center that was established in 1892. The 30-foot octagonal tower is of wooden construction, like many of the beacons used to guide shipping on this long, sheltered arm of the Pacific, whose coastline extends 100 miles into Washington State and provides its major deep-water ports.

Reef, Caisson & Screwpile Lighthouses

A new era of lighthouse construction began to emerge in the decade prior to the Civil War. Technological advances enabled engineers to design more sophisticated structures in locations previously considered unsuitable for building. For the first time, sturdy foundations could be laid offshore using several different methods. Known as the reef, caisson, or screwpile types of lighthouses, these structures were designed to stand in the water and on reefs. Naturally, they had to offer less resistance to the waves than heavier structures like the octagonal and pyramidal towers.

The British pioneer in this area was Alexander Mitchell, a blind engineer who designed the first iron screwpile lighthouse for the Malpin Sands, in the mouth of the Thames River, in 1838. His innovations included three-foot bars that were screwed into sand or rock to fasten the lighthouse foundation securely. Mitchell patented his invention in 1842, and word of this ingenious method of building on treacherous reefs soon spread to North America.

Subsequent tests by trial and error led to the development of the pneumatic pile and the caisson. The former method involved sinking submarine piles through the use of atmospheric pressure, and the latter, pumping air into large cylinders in which men could work underwater to clear away existing obstacles. This allowed for laying caisson (or crib) foundations on which granite towers were built.

Minots Ledge Light, near Cohasset, Massachusetts, just south of Boston, was the first screwpile lighthouse to be built in the United States. It went into service in 1850, but was torn apart by a violent storm the following year. The Lighthouse Board made elaborate preparations before building a second lighthouse on the treacherous reef: their 97-foot-tall granite structure still stands, having weathered innumerable storms over the years.

In the southern United States, Army Lieutenant George G. Meade supervised the construction of a pile lighthouse on Florida's Carysfort Reef in 1852. Still in service today, the spider-legged tower spawned a chain of screwpile buildings, especially in Chesapeake Bay and on the Gulf Coast. Lieutenant Meade would rise to the rank of general and command Union forces at the crucial Battle of Gettysburg in 1863.

By the time the Civil War ended, the United States led the way in the use of two forms: the straight-pile and the screwpile lighthouse. Minots Ledge was an excellent example of the straight-pile structure, while Brandywine Shoal Lighthouse in Delaware Bay, built in 1850, was the first true screwpile (also called bay or harbor) lighthouse in North America. All of the screwpile lights in the United States were one-story wooden towers, ranging in shape from octagonal to square or rectangular. Only five of these lights remain today, four in Chesapeake Bay and one in Mobile Bay.

Special conditions demanded ingenuity on the part of architects and engineers. Marshall Point Light at Port Clyde, Maine, stands just off the coast, to which it is joined by a wooden bridge resting on granite piles. Guarding the entrance to the harbor of Newport, Rhode Island, Castle Hill Light was built into the side of a rock ledge at the water's edge. Both of these lights were built in locations that would have made construction impossible before the 1850s.

Just offshore of Fishers Island, New York, stands one of the most remarkable feats of nineteenth-century American engineering: Race Rock Light. Built over seven years by Francis Hopkinson Smith (who also designed the foundations for the Statue of Liberty) and Thomas A. Scott, the light stands on a reef notorious for the ferocity of its tides and waves. Many ships were wrecked there prior to the light's installation.

Eight miles northwest of Race Rock stands the New London Ledge Light, with its highly unusual design in the French Second Empire style. Although New London Harbor Light had guarded the west side of the mouth of the Thames River for more than a century, mariners complained that it was inadequate, because of the large reef in the middle of the harbor. Finished in 1909, New London Ledge Light stands on a square concrete foundation and pier a mile from shore. It almost appears to float in the middle of the river, giving a very unusual character to the city's harbor.

Twenty miles west of New London Ledge Light is the Saybrook Breakwater Light, at the end of a long breakwater that juts directly south from Lynde Point Light. Known to locals as the "Outer Light," it is short and squat, resembling a fortress. This may help to account for the fact that it survived the terrible hurricane of 1938.

Maine's distinctive Portland Breakwater Light now stands on a landfill and exemplifies the cone-shaped, prefabricated cast-iron lighthouses that were built in New England between 1870 and 1920. Its elegant Greek Revival style gives little clue to the strength of its tubular cast-iron foundation. In the Ocean State of Rhode Island, the 38-foot octagonal tower of Newport Harbor Light, built after the Civil War on the northern tip of Goat Island, is the third beacon at the harbor entrance. Its rough-cut granite-block construction, painted white, was common in Rhode Island, where granite was quarried at Westerly.

Innovative lighthouses that were erected on the Great Lakes include Round Island Light and Spectacle Reef. The latter was designed by Major O.M. Poe, who had been chief engineer on General William T. Sherman's Civil-War march through Georgia. All of Poe's formidable engineering talents were called upon during the four-year construction of Spectacle Reef. Built at almost the same time as Race Rock Light, this beacon stands as another milestone in nineteenth-century American engineering.

Designers and engineers like Smith and Poe may well have believed that their newly developed construction methods would prevail for centuries. However, twentieth-century technologies would soon lead to the construction of lighter towers and electric signals that would obviate the need for such heroic feats of engineering as Race Rock and Spectacle Reef—and the grueling task of manning lonely lighthouses to protect the mariners along our shores.

Previous pages: Tarrytown Harbor Light, New York.

Marshall Point Light

Port Clyde, St. George, Maine

Marshall Point stands at the southern tip of the St. George peninsula as it juts into Muscongus Bay, off the coast of central Maine. In 1832 a 19-foot rubblestone tower was built at Marshall Point to warn sailors of the dangers as they approached the eastern side of Port Clyde Harbor. The original lighthouse had to be taken down in 1857, because the mortar holding the fieldstones in place had given way under constant pressure from waves. The new tower, erected in the same year, is 31 feet tall, equipped with a fifth-order Fresnel lens which has its focal plane 30 feet above sea level. A wooden bridge, resting on granite piles, connects the isolated tower to the mainland. The station was automated in 1971, and the land was leased to the St. George Historical Society, which has opened part of the keeper's dwelling as a lighthouse museum. The lighthouse remains the point of departure for the ferry to Monhegan Island. Marshall Point Light boasts a proud record: Charles Skinner served as keeper between July 6, 1874, and May 7, 1919, the longest tenure in the history of the U.S. Lighthouse Service.

Castle Hill Light

Castle Hill, Rhode Island (Opposite)

In 1524 the Italian sailor Giovanni da Verrazano (financed by the king of France) sailed past the spot of present-day Castle Hill Light as he entered Narragansett Bay. Verrazano spent fifteen days in the bay area, and reported favorably on both the region's fertility and the beauty of the indigenous people. He and his men found plums, hazel and beech nuts, and "apples worthy of Lucullus." As he departed, Verrazano noted the splendid location of Narragansett Bay and observed prophetically that it could shelter a fleet of great size. There is still controversy on the question of whether Verrazano saw a stone tower (which some archaeologists claim is the stone tower on the hill at Newport), or whether his map notation merely indicated the presence of a native village there.

Verrazano's prophecies came true in the nineteenth century, when Narragansett Bay became a center for the U.S. Navy. The town of Newport itself became the site of some of the largest, most beautiful and most expensive homes of wealthy Americans (the Vanderbilt mansion, "The Breakers," is one of the most grandiose). One wealthy resident of the bay was the famous naturalist Alexander Agassiz (1835–1910), who steadfastly refused to allow townspeople to build a lighthouse on his property. The need was evident, since the point at Castle Hill—just across from and north of **Beavertail Light** (pages 44–45)—was vital to the guidance of sailors approaching Newport Harbor. In response to Agassiz' refusal, steamboat companies painted the rocky cliffs at Castle Hill white for the safety of their vessels at night.

Finally, in 1890, the light was constructed overlooking Newport's harbor entrance, to guide vessels along the eastern channel of Narragansett Bay. The magnificent, rugged granite structure is in the influential Richardsonian Romanesque style, and it is believed possible that the renowned architect Henry Hobson Richardson himself (1838–1886) may have designed the tower. At this time his Trinity Church, in Boston, was considered by other architects the finest building in the nation.

The sturdy masonry structure was emplaced in a rock ledge at waterside. The upper half of the tower is painted white, and the stone brackets that once held the fog bell are visible below the gallery. Originally, the station had a keeper's house and several outbuildings, but they were damaged so severely by the hurricane of 1938 that the Coast Guard did not rebuild them. Only the tower remained, commanding a beautiful view of historic Newport and its harbor, where the French fleet sent to assist American colonists in the Revolutionary War was anchored in 1780–81.

Castle Hill is still a working aid to navigation, equipped with a fifth-order lens that flashes a red light at 42 feet above sea level and the fog horn that replaced the original bell. The light was automated by the Coast Guard in 1957.

Race Rock Light

On Race Rock Reef, 0.6 miles southwest of Fishers Island, New York

Built between 1871 and 1878, Race Rock Light is one of the triumphs of American engineering and design. Race Rock Reef is a notoriously dangerous set of rocks off the coast of Fishers Island on Long Island Sound: eight ships were lost there between 1829 and 1837 alone. Francis Hopkinson Smith (1838–1915) was chosen to engineer construction of a light on the reef. He had already built several breakwaters in other locations and would eventually lay the foundations for the Statue of Liberty. Smith and Captain Thomas Albertson Scott, the construction foreman, took seven long years to lay the massive masonry foundations on the reef; once that was accomplished, the tower and keeper's quarters took an additional nine months to complete. The granite tower stands 67 feet above the water, and its fourth-order lens is visible for up to 14 miles. The U.S. Coast Guard automated the light in 1979.

New London Ledge Light
New London, Connecticut

At first sight, New London Ledge Light makes the onlooker wonder whether he or she is seeing a lighthouse or a Victorian mansion adrift on the ocean. The square, three-story brick structure has granite trim and a mansard roof in the then-fashionable Second Empire style. The Lighthouse Board ordered construction in 1909, because the **New London Harbor Light** (page 49) was judged inadequate to the needs of the harbor by many captains. Since New London Harbor Light guarded the western side of the mouth of the Thames River, the new light was built roughly halfway between the eastern and western sides. The tower and lantern, equipped with a fourth-order Fresnel lens, rose from the center of the roof, creating an appearance very different from that of most contemporary Connecticut lights. The Ledge Light soon took over many of the duties formerly assigned to the New London Harbor Light. In 1987 the Ledge Light was automated. Still in use today, it has been leased by the U. S. Coast Guard to the New London Ledge Lighthouse Foundation. Many Coast Guard keepers believed that the lighthouse was haunted: stories still circulate about a ghost called "Ernie," a keeper who committed suicide at the light after learning that his wife had run off with the captain of the ferry boat to Block Island.

Saybrook Breakwater Light
Old Saybrook, Connecticut *(Opposite)*

"When daylight came at last, what we saw seemed more like a dream than reality. There was nothing around the tower except the battery house, and even that was badly out of shape." So wrote keeper Sidney Gross on the morning after the terrible hurricane of 1938. Known to locals as the "Outer Light," the Saybrook Breakwater Light was built in 1886. The cast-iron conical tower stands at the end of a jetty extending south from **Lynde Point Light** (page 48) into Long Island Sound. The hurricane of 1938 ripped away the platform that encircled the beacon, and storm tides dislodged some of the granite blocks from the jetty itself. Keeper Sidney Gross reported that water was pouring through the second-story windows by 6 PM on the night that the storm hit.

Portland Breakwater Light
Portland, Maine *(Below)*

The first lighthouse at Portland Breakwater was built in 1855: octagonal and made of wood, it stood at the outer end of the 1,900-foot breakwater. The lighthouse soon succumbed to dampness, and in 1875 it was replaced by a small cast-iron structure that served until 1942. By that time, two shipyards had been built, changing the configuration of the harbor, and the light was no longer needed. Resembling a small Greek monument, complete with Corinthian columns, the structure has been restored and is now owned by the City of Portland.

Newport Harbor Light
Goat Island, Newport, Rhode Island

"The mouth of the haven lies open to the south half a league broad, and being entered within it between the east and the north, it stretches twelve leagues, where it becomes broader and broader." Explorer Giovanni da Verrazano wrote these words in 1524, after he and his crew had entered Narragansett Bay and what is now the harbor of Newport, Rhode Island.

Newport Harbor Light stands at the northern tip of Goat Island, just beneath Newport Bridge and covering the entrance to Newport Harbor. It is the last of three lights in this vicinity and is still active, although the bridge itself has diminished the light's importance as a navigational aid. In 1823 a 30-foot octagonal tower was erected on Goat Island, intended to guide ships safely to anchor. This first

tower was superseded by a lighthouse built on a nearby breakwater in 1838. The original tower remained unlit for thirteen years, until it was moved 10 miles to Prudence Island in Portsmouth. Lit there in 1852, and known as the Sandy Point Light, it is Rhode Island's oldest standing lighthouse, and its bird-cage lantern is unique among the Ocean State's legendary beacons.

In 1865 a new tower with keeper's dwelling attached was built at the tip of Goat Island. The 35-foot octagonal lighthouse was made of granite blocks painted white. Soon after the construction of this beacon, Goat Island became the site of a naval torpedo factory. The dwelling was rammed by a submarine in 1922, and damaged so severely that it was razed by the Bureau of Lighthouses. The lighthouse remained and was eventually automated, in 1963. Recently, the area between the coast and the lighthouse was filled in, creating a small grassy park.

Hillsboro Inlet Light
Deerfield, Florida (Left)

The iron skeleton tower of the Hillsboro Inlet Light was first displayed at the 1904 Exposition in St. Louis. Today, its second-order Fresnel lens is 136 feet above sea level and emits a light measuring 5.5 million candlepower, making this one of the most powerful lights in the South. Located on the north side of Hillsboro Inlet, which is midway between Fort Lauderdale and Boca Raton, the octagonal pyramidal tower has a metal cylinder housing the stairs. The lighthouse marks the northern limit of the Florida Reef, an underwater coral formation that parallels the lower east coast of the state. Now automated, the light serves both as a coastal navigational aide and a guide to the inlet, which has become an increasingly busy waterway in the second half of the twentieth century.

Fort Point Light
San Francisco, California *(Above)*

Now located in the Fort Point National Historic Site, directly beneath the south anchorage of the Golden Gate Bridge, the lighthouse crowns Fort Winfield Scott, constructed in 1853 to defend San Francisco Bay. This is the third lighthouse on the bluff formerly known as Battery Point: the two constructed in the 1850s were torn down, the first to build Fort Winfield Scott, and the second to extend its seawall. The existing metal tower above the fort's northwest corner was erected in 1864 with a fifth-order Fresnel lens and deactivated in 1934. It has been restored since 1970, when Congress established the point as a national historic site.

Drum Point Light
Calvert County, Maryland *(Opposite, below)*

The Lighthouse Board decided in 1864 that a beacon was needed at the entrance to Maryland's Patuxent River. Surprisingly, it was not until 1883 that the board took action. In that year, the screwpile lighthouse was built in 10 feet of water and about 100 yards off the point. Constructed in just thirty-three days, the light was secured to the river bottom by flanges 3 feet across. A one-and-a-half story hexagonal keeper's dwelling was built on top of the platform. The focal plane of the lens was 47 feet above sea level. By the early 1960s, the light stood completely out of the water at low tide. In 1962 the Coast Guard decommissioned it, and it remained inactive for twelve years. The Calvert County Historical Society moved the structure 2 miles upriver to the Calvert Marine Museum in 1975.

Round Island Light

St. Ignace, Michigan

Although it was decommissioned in 1947, Round Island Light is now the most photographed lighthouse in the Great Lakes region: thousands of tourists pass it as they take hydroplane ferries between St. Ignace and Mackinaw City to Mackinac Island. The island is on the eastern side of the Straits of Mackinac, separating Lakes Michigan and Huron. Round Island Light was built in 1895 to mark the dangerous shoals around the channel between Round and Mackinac Islands. The two-and-one-half story keeper's dwelling was constructed of red brick with a square tower rising above the roofline. Three full-time keepers manned the station for more than fifty years, working in shifts around the clock. The light was automated in 1924 and taken out of service in 1947. The structure fell into a condition of near-ruin before a local restoration group mobilized to save it in the 1970s. Today, the lighthouse is listed on the National Register of Historic Places and serves as a vivid reminder of the beauty of these historic structures and the important role they have played in maritime commerce on the Great Lakes.

Spectacle Reef Light
Cheboygan, Lake Huron, Michigan

The conical tower of Spectacle Reef Light stands 95 feet tall and its pale sandy color makes it easy to distinguish from other lighthouses in the area. Built of limestone transported from Marblehead, Ohio, the lighthouse took four years to erect. It is located on a submerged limestone reef in northern Lake Huron, approximately 11 miles east of the Straits of Mackinac. Built between 1870 and 1874, Spectacle Reef has a base 32 feet in diameter and 11 feet below water level. The 95-foot tower's focal plane is 97 feet above the lake. A masterpiece of engineering, Spectacle Reef Light is securely bolted to the foundation rock by long metal rods. Spectacle Reef Light was the Lake Huron-featured lighthouse on the Great Lakes Lighthouse series of stamps issued by the U.S. Postal Service in 1995. The light is now automated.

Index & Acknowledgements

Index

Acknowledgements

The publisher would like to thank the following individuals for their assistance in the preparation of this book: Charles J. Ziga, art director; Wendy Ciaccia Eurell, graphic designer; Sara Hunt and Robin Langley Sommer, editors; Nicola J. Gillies, production editor; Charles F. Ziga for his assistance on photographic shoots; Jay Hyland of The Lighthouse Preservation Society. All photographs are © Charles J. Ziga except the following: © Calvert Marine Museum, Solomons, MD: 92b; © Robert Drapala: 31; © Jae Greer: 42; © Margaret Harris: 9, 10, 23, 35; © Hiawatha National Forest 94; © James Hyland: 32, 34, 44, 92t, 95; © Chris Mills: 8, 25, 51; © Mississippi Gulf Coast CVB: 33; © Ottawa County Visitors Bureau: 28; © Lee Radzak: 56–57; © Dick Roberts: 88; © John Sylvester: 30, 50, 52–53.